Splashes Through Life

Jeanice Cummings

CHERISHED WORDS

PUBLISHING

Splashes Through Life

Copyright © 2024 by Jeanice Cummings
Cherished Words Publishing
ISBN: (sc):   978-1-963917-27-7
ISBN: (hb):   978-1-963917-28-4
ISBN: (ebook): 978-1-963917-29-1

Library of Congress Control Number: 2024912263

Printed in the United States of America

Contents

Introduction

Splashes through Life, is a soulful search of a young girl and her progression through the different stages of life. She has journeyed far with no sense of direction and awakens from her cocoon late in life. Just like a butterfly emerges the young girl stops to recall the splashes of her life that she now remembers. These memories have allowed her to express her feelings through her poetry while gaining a sense of peace, tranquility and direction in her life. It is my sincere hope and desire that this anthology of poems will touch the reader in a most positive way as it has done for the author.

Pseudonym Jeanice Cummings

Simply Moving

The living organisms of the body yearn to be nurtured, fed and loved. Simply through moving swaying to the rhythm of the soul. Unleashing the strength and power within. Simply moving eliminating all stagnated energy that's stuck with nowhere to go. Energy just trapped in the body, craving to be let free from being a hostage. Bring the body out of captivity; let it breathe the fresh air of life. Simply move it, feed it with love, simply move it right now, this very moment. Get up and move stretch bend. Simply moving demonstrates love and respect for the body and propels it to give us the same love in return.

Yearning for Approval

Talking way too much, sharing thoughts, talents and ideas with others. After speaking these ideas to others they rarely manifests into success. I have what it takes, but I keep yearning and yearning for approval. Having a need to be validated by someone and told that I am really okay.

I feel never felt quite good enough, smart enough, pretty enough, sexy enough or confident enough. I just kept on yearning and yearning for approval.

Whatever gave me the idea that I was not quite good enough, smart enough, pretty enough, sexy enough or confident enough? Ideas embedded into my consciousness and the tapes keep playing over and over again. Greatness does reside within me. But I just keep yearning and yearning for approval.

Life passes by as quickly as a moving freight train and there's no time to think negative thoughts. Time has no foreseeable ending for me or for any one of us.

I do know that I do have the power to be who I am destined and created to be. I need only believe in me and give me the approval that I have been seeking and yearning. What I am searching for ironically is yearning to be set free inside of me.

Rushing and Rushing

Rushing and rushing around; from dusk till dawn a lot of the time. Rushing around and often losing oneself in the maze of life. Just reacting and not thinking, going day-by-day on automatic pilot with the mind not fully engaged.

Rushing and rushing around not remembering to say, "I love you," to the people who matter in life. Unconsciously forgetting to acknowledge one another, never looking up to say hello. not thinking that someone could use a kind word or smile today. Rushing and rushing around never pausing to look up at the sky. Never stopping to appreciate and admire the innocence of a child nor the delicacy of their being.

Rushing and rushing around: not valuing the wisdom of our elders. Our ancestors paid the price for us to have a say. Rushing and rushing around never even stopping to breathe, just runnning from day to day. Rushing and rushing : never reaching a true destination. Rushing so fast and letting life pass, just pass-by.

Night Birds

The birds seem to talk more to each other at night; while a less noisy environment echoes over the land. If the birds were to speak during the day, the activities of the day would drown them out with the sounds of the day.

The birds are quite talkative at night, it could be that they are discussing me, or maybe you, or maybe even about their day? Who really knows?

The Night Birds may be freer at night. Free from the hustle and bustle of the day. Free to speak only to one another. Humans are too busy doing life to listen. So the birds talk amongst themselves at night. In the stillness of the night listen for them and you will hear them; I surely have. They are Night Birds talking at night while the world is fast asleep.

To Savone from Gwam-ma

When she smiles the dimples
in her cheeks light
us as she says, "Hi Gwam-ma."
Then she runs and jumps
into my arms and says,
"I love you Gwam-ma.
In my mind it's as
if she was always in my life.
She brings a special meaning
to what it feels
like for me to be a, Gwam-ma.

Teach Me and Keep Me

Keep me and teach me Great Spirit how to not be cruel and mean to others. As I have to face life and all its adversities, may I remember that others share the same fate. Keep me Great Spirit, from trying to control everyone and every situation. I am but a tiny speckle in this world and all I need to do in this life is to treat everyone with true compassion and devotion. Teach and help me to remember that we all belong and are part of the web of life. My calling in this life is to consent to share and to give love to whoever is accepting. Keep me and teach me how to redirect others from tainting my spirit. Keep me and teach me to love without limits. Keep me and teach me.

Cry Together

When we cry together, we can mourn together for all the loves we have lost. If losing the love of someone hurts so deeply inside, then why must we ever love? Happiness is but a fleeting moment in life, why then do we dwell on insignificant things? When we cry together we share the love we have for one another and nothing in the world can erase this. Living is never a problem when an appreciation for it is acknowledged and felt. Why then do we not do what it takes to enjoy the greatest love of all? Why then is there hesitation to give and accept love? Should there be? I think not. When we cry together we reach into the distant future with a better understanding of its real meaning. The fact that life is short makes it even more valuable. Love and pain or synonymous at times. When we cry together we can love together, and give that love to those who really matter.

The Close of the Day

The moon seems to rotate as I sit on a plane bound for Seattle. I wonder how many others are watching from the air or the ground. The orange like patterns that engulf the circle of the moon vibrates rays that are everlasting or so it would seem or be.

While I watch the moon the color does not change. But when I turn around its fully white with tiny speckles of gray. The darkness that surrounds the moon lets me know that the close of the day is here.

What did the day bring to you? Can you really remember? Or does life pass by so quickly the memory of the day is dim, as is the quality of our life that we have become enslaved too. It's hard to remember each and every day to thank God, for even having the chance to see the close of the day.

Such Innocence

Sitting in the car sensing the sun warming the right side of my face. The left side of my face is breezy cold rather like an autumn day. Parents are here at the park by the lake, pushing and thrusting their children in the swings as they push them upward towards the sky. How high can they go? Some kids are on the slides, sliding down without a care in the world. Such beauty! Such divine innocence! The children seem to have such a love and enthusiasm for life.

My eyes become fixated on a beautiful little girl around the age of two. Her mother holds tightly to her as she pretends to slide down the slide to the ground. Not really sliding down on her own she needs her mother's help. She is dressed in a pair of blue jeans, a purple sweat shirt and a stripped red and white knit cap. I laughed to myself thinking that she could easily be mistaken for one of Santa's elves. What beauty and such divine innocence.

As I listen to her hypnotic laugh, her face lights up and gleams with a joyous expression in the midday sun. Such beauty and such divine innocence she is.

My Special Place

I travel up a dirt road where the dust separates from the ground and dissipates into the air. The weeds on the sides of the road are unkempt. But I don't mind because I am going to the most beautiful place in the world, "My grandfathers farm." It feeds me emotionally with love and makes me feel safe. It nourishes my body and makes me feel unbroken and complete.

My grandfather's farm and all the wonderful smells of livestock, plants feed and mud. And the sounds of chattering birds and animal noises. My grandfathers farm; the only place where I could find solace and run free like the antelope in the fields. Oh how I miss my grandfather; his wisdom, peace, love and gentle ways. Grandfather, the time we spent together was much more precious than gold. But God took you home because he needed you more.

Here Comes Francis

"Story of a little girl who talked too much"

When I was in the Fourth Grade, I was talking to a friend of mine named Mary about a girl named Francis. Days and weeks passed by without incident. One day on the gravel ridden playground by the slides, Francis comes towards me with a caravan of friends.

Francis exclaims, "Mary told me what you said about me. "What can I do? My heart is pounding, I was sweating and shaking. I hoped no one noticed. I didn't know if I could whip Francis. I can't just run away.

I know. I'll tell Francis that I'm hurt because she felt I would say such things about her. And if she want to fight me, "I will."

Francis hesitated and thought for awhile. Oops the bell rang and it was time to go back inside. The funniest thing about the whole incident is, "I actually forgot what it was I said about Francis."

If You Woke Up Fat Today

If you woke up fat today how would you feel and what would you do? How would your family and friends accept you this way? Or would they have a long list of diets and exercise programs to refer you too?

If you woke up fat today and could no longer fit into your classy clothes, and could no longer poke fun at others, what would you do? What if people gawked at you and turned their noses up at you in disgust? If you woke up fat today what would you say to the small person who mirrors their impression of you in their face, and wears it like a neon sign on their foreheads? All I have to say is, you better hope that you don't wake up fat today. So no more advice and diets please. For if you woke up fat today, you would be just another fat person. The truth is that you really don't know what it's like to be fat do you? So don't make fun.

Unwrap the Images

Unwrap the images that are instilled in my mind of the places I have visited and those which I have yet to explore. Unwrap the images of the day that is past and the lessons Learned. I guess I am expected to use these lessons to improve my life? But I honestly don't know what steps to take to get started. Lessons serve little purpose unless we use them in life today. Unwrap the images and look inward to the spirit located inside of you. There you will find all of the answers you seek. Where all is eloquent and the images become real not only in the mind but in the heart too.

In the Wee Hours of the Morning

In the Wee hours of the morning when I awake to stillness and calm, and almost everyone is asleep.

I ask the Great Spirit to bless me with humility and love. Love for my fellow humans, love of nature and its creation, love for myself and all my imperfections of which are often harder to love.

In the Wee hours of the morning when I scan my mind to reflect on my activities for the day I pray for patience and peace that I might offer it to others.

In the Wee hours of the morning after I pray and let go of my own expectations. I marinade over my decision to get up; so I turn off my alarm clock. I understand fully that everything I do serves a purpose.

In the Wee hours of the morning while some are sleeping, I am holding a private conversation with just Spirit and me.

Another Lifetime

I really don't have another lifetime to be who I want to be. To live the way I want to live, to speak what I feel and to walk tall and firm. I really don't have another lifetime to hide my feelings and bury them deep inside my soul. I really don't have another lifetime to miss any small portion of life. I really don't have another life time to laugh at my own jokes and to sing my own song, and to write my own lyrics. I only have this one lifetime. So I am going to live for today in this lifetime. This is the only Lifetime I have.

Incognito

Traveling incognito she is, with a black hat drooped over her head, her face her identity unknown. Traveling incognito, barely raising her head only looking down or up into the crevices of her flop hat that reflects a shaded space shielded from the light.

Traveling incognito no one knows who she is, nor does she seem to want them to recognize who she is. Inactively sitting in her essence with presence; captivated by time in her own space. Traveling incognito she is, feeling no stress at all, besides no really knows her anyway. Traveling incognito she is free to discover. Free to be unknown, free to go unrecognized and free to travel incognito.

The First Day

Today is the beginning of the first day of my life. Today I get a chance to start all over again forgetting about my mistakes from yesterday.

Today I forgive myself for the things I didn't know and still don't know. Forgiving myself for the hurt I may have unknowing imposed on anyone.

Today is the beginning of the first day of my life. Today I will follow my heart and surrender to my higher power to be led by faith. I know that I will be ok because spirit resides in me and is the core of who I am and who I desire to be.

Today is the beginning of the first day of my life and I am truly blessed to have another chance. I live life each and every day just like it's the first day of my life all over again.

Make Believe

As she sits on the dry summer grass with a pen and paper in her hand she wonders, "Will I ever be the poet I dreamed I would be?

Will I ever be asked to tell the story of my life again and again and without one getting bored? Will my fans run after me in the streets hoping to get an autograph of two?

Will people stand and applaud me for the words that I speak? As I stand on the platform today, I take a bow and look over the crowd. I can't help but remember, the little girl who sat on the dry grass with a pen and paper in her hand, who use to make believe she was a poet. And now guess what? She really is.

The Sun

If I were the sun, I would shine down on earth and erase sadness from the hearts of mankind. Shine brightly when people could not see any light. Be there for them any time of the day. Emulate light for them for as long as they need it. Maybe then they could see all the goodness that life has to offer. If I were the sun I'd work all day and all night until the time has come for me to disappear in the night. Many days I would shine down on earth so others can be uplifted and warmed by the sun. I would share sunlight to light up the hearts of men and peace would reign forever if I were the sun.

The Smell of Fall

I love this time of the year, when the morning is semi-dark and the leaves on the trees slowly fall to the ground.

It's the smell of fall. I can't see the wind but I feel it as it penetrates the first layer of my skin. It's the smell of fall which has me recall my younger years; when at times I felt excited and overwhelmed with the joy of being me. Such a wonderfully happy time of the year.

It's the smell of fall that starts me remembering the holiday festivities. I still have these splashes of nostalgia when I smell the evergreen trees and the smell of fresh oranges and apples.

It's the smell of fall that helps me to remember, to value each and every fall year-after-year. Isn't this the sweetest blessing of all?

Are you really in Charge?

It's easy to believe that you are in charge of a person over the phone, when you are rude and insensitive and argue disrespectfully. The people you are speaking with, remember are your customers. Without them you would not have a job. Or did you forget?

Why you choose to speak to me in downgraded manner is a mystery to me, when all I ask for is kindness from you. It's easy to exercise power over me when I am at a disadvantage and my money is low.

Does asking for payment arrangements motivate you to mention a slow payment history? What makes you believe that you have a right to lecture me about paying my bills on time. Is there a reason you want to make me feel bad? Or are you just in a bad mood and taking it out on me?

Are you really in charge or just taking this time to make yourself feel good at my expense? Anyone can be in charge over the phone but the real test is, are you in charge of your own life? Being in charge does not afford you the right to be mean to me. Kindness is free and there is no charge.

Aging Too Fast

God stop me from aging too fast I don't mean on the surface I mean internally. God, if you would just stop me from complaining too much about my aches and pains cause everyone has them. God, stop me from restricting myself by not being involved in my life.

God, stop me from gossiping and being mean to anyone. Stop me from taking my loved ones for granted, they are the people who bring love into my life. Help me to compliment them anytime of the day even when they are not so good, let me show them love.

God, stop me from focusing on the small insignificant things that really don't matter. And stop me from aging too fast by not sharing the love I have with the people who can use it, and with the people I love and who love me. God stop me from aging too fast . . . .

The Indigent Patient

They call her an indigent patient because she has no medical insurance and can't afford to purchase any because she has three children and a grandchild to care for. They have insurance but she does not.

They make her wait to be seen for hours, like all she has to do is to wait in the doctor's office. "She's poor and has nothing better to do," is what they seem to think but not speak.

They call her an indigent patient when they holler out in the waiting room in front of other patients, "she does not have any insurance." As if she does not already feel bad enough the office worker asks her can she pay on a sliding scale and she agrees knowing that the bill will eventually wind up in collections.

They call her an indigent patient and treat her as such by not looking her in her face just looking through her or away from her.

She sees their perceptions of her in their faces. It's a face she has seen so many times but she holds her composure. She cringes and exhales and says to herself, "I won't be indigent forever, but these people will always be cruel and mean; that will remain unchanged.

Pine Cones

Pine cones glued to the branches of a tree limb. Each day they detach themselves more and more and drop to the ground. What if they are not ready to detach themselves? Do you think that Mother Nature will afford them a longer time to stay on the branches?

Are pine cone ejected after aging a certain time and are there any exceptions to the rule? As the time draws nearer for the pine cone to disconnect from the tree branch, does it suffer anxiety at leaving its comfortable place in the tree?

For the pine cones that has been attached to a tree for so long, it most likely seems like such a long and scary way down to the ground. Pine cones just lay there until they eventually evaporate into the ground. They leave a fresh clean smell in the environment and I'm glad that the fall down and bless us with their presence.

Wounds

Wounds, deep wounds which cannot be expressed only felt. Wounds, deep wounds which did not come from me. I have not created or lived these wounds in my life.

How did I become wounded and never live it? Where did these wounds come from? Wounds, deep wounds cry out loudly to be healed. My ancestors request that I release these wounds from the bondage of their untold secrets. These secret wounds.

Wounds, deep wounds which should be laid to rest. Sleep mysterious wounds and return to me no more. As I speak these wounds out loud they will depart from me. At last my ancestors can rest; I have done what they never had the chance to do and they are pleased.

A Silenced Heart

I don't seem to have the same longing and hunger to understand my purpose anymore. My heart has become silenced.

My heart is anesthetized as I go through the motions of my day lifeless. I am dazed by not knowing my real purpose. I feel sad it hurts me deeply not to know my purpose. Let me breathe fresh new life into me. Please gift me with faith and the innocence of a child devoid of all the scars of my past.

Let me sour like an eagle in the clouds. Let my spirit be free once again, give me back my desire to understand my purpose. Help me and let me understand why I am here on earth. Let my heart speak to me once again. A silenced heart has no real purpose or destination. Awaken my heart so that I might understand and appreciate why I was chosen to be on earth.

A Remainder Called Death

Not many think about death until it comes to their doorstep. I never really thought about it or associated my friend with death until death came knocking at Shelia's doorstep. I am not sure if she was prepared to hear the dreaded knock of death come calling. As a matter of fact, I doubt if she was ready to make her transition, and as for me I was not ready for her to leave this earth.

I miss her smiling face, our gossip sessions and her laughter, but cancer came knocking and it was a loud and boisterous knock. I doubt if Shelia was ready to go but she didn't seem to struggle to stay here in the present. She had little motivation to fight the cancer. Maybe she knew it was a losing battle that she could not win.

Shelia, my friend may you sing with the angels and dance till you can't dance anymore and be merry. I know you will add a positive presence in the spiritual world. Your essence and generosity have no boundary and words can't express how strongly you are missed.

The Inside of Me

The outer layer of who I am is not really the essence of who I am. It likens to the outside cover of an egg, a peanut shell, a turtle and chocolate covered candy. The outside layer is just a mere image of who I really am.

Once the shell is exposed the entire valuable me inside is exposed for the entire world to see. Who I am today is artistically created in God's image. I am chosen to be here.

The inner part of who I am is really me and I no longer choose to hide myself in a shell of defeat. The outside and inside of me is all of who I am. I commit to myself to allow the inside of me to radiate out for the entire world to see. For the inside of me is not all that I am. It is the real me.

Trying to Separate Friends

Friends, people are always trying to separate them; lovers, relatives, friends it doesn't matter. People appear to be perplexed with the fact that caring about a friend is as important as any other type of intimate relationship. Consumed with jealousy and envy some are angered because love feelings boarder on the same feelings we have for our friends.

There is really no competition where one or the other must win. Friends or shall I say, "special friends" are always there when needed to give you a lift. Friends tells you good and tough things because there is a knowledge that it will help us grow. They tolerate people in your life regardless of their personal feelings.

Real friends remind us of the many good things in life after the world has deflated our ego. I'll share everything with my friend, while my lover has my heart; my friend has my dedication and respect. Nothing can really separate friendship unless the season has ended and you part ways. True friends actually do stand the test of time and no one can separate them.

Chasing Rainbows

I've spent much of my life chasing rainbows; looking here and there with not a rainbow in sight. Going too fast on life's merry go round, I just can't seem to stop so I can get off.

Chasing rainbows and speeding through life like a jet plane. I have no conscious thoughts, I just move from day to day in a fog.

Chasing rainbows this is not what I thought my life would be. Not long ago I saw a little girl sitting at her favorite hideaway spot envisioning and dreaming large with no limits. Life seems to have faded those dreams after becoming an adult.

I somehow lost the vision. Going through life enslaved by an economy brought about by heartless and greedy people. This was not my dream. I still believe that rainbows are out there just waiting to transform my life.

Through the Eyes of a Teenager

The police came to our house today, what will our neighbors say? My step-dad hit my mom today and all us kids are really scared. You'd Think he would think of how we felt, but he doesn't really care.

From day-to-day we never know what will set him off. He starts by telling her how dumb and stupid she is to be his wife. Is this the reason that she lets him ruin all our lives?

He has the job and all the money so we must depend on him. He buys everything and I'm so sick of his cheap taste. You would think he would ask her what she wants, but for him it seems like such a waste.

Sometimes when were at dinner I sit nervously by; my stomach is so nervous I want to find a place to hide. Tonight is Friday night, he dressing and he's on the town again. Why in the hell did he get married? His disrespectful behavior is such a sin. He'll return in the morning and the fighting will begin.

Tonight our house is a circus, but there will be no funny clowns. My mom will wind up battered and all our lives torn down. She says today, "We're leaving," although she said this many times before. But for some unknown reasons we never make it to the door.

Our lives return to normal, but we're deeply hurt inside. For we know by Next weekend the police will come again.

A Plane in the Distant Clouds

I see a plane in the distant clouds. From where I am it looks like a bird as it disappears in the clouds. The clouds are a medium dark blue, almost a turquoise in color, as shades of blue shine through the haze.

God, I won't forget to thank you, today and every day. Now I notice another plane floating with the clouds, moving, merging together as one. The plane suddenly fades into the clouds almost as quickly as it comes into view.

The plane has a destination as it soars across the sky. A plane in the distant clouds. From where I stand it looks like a bird, but it's not it's a plane in the far-away clouds.

Ritual to Honor Self

Spirit God, I am grateful for everything you have given to me. I honor who I am and appreciate what I have become. And the road has not been easy having encountered many crooked turns and stales.

I ask you today to help me remain humble, centered and powerful in who I am, for you have created me, you are my designer. And you designed me with precision and perfection.

I pray that I will not let anyone destroy the beautiful spirit you have bestowed upon me. When a confusing situation attempts to control and consume me. I will let it pass through me to the ground and dissipate into the soil. Let it nourish and fertilize the earth for the goodness of all.

I give praise to you Spirit God, and ask for your blessings and love forever more. I henceforth honor and love myself for who I am today, tomorrow, and always.

If I Raise My Voice

If I raise my voice out loud will I be listened too? Will my feelings be discounted or rationalized with words such as; she is angry, bitter, wounded, spiteful or void of any understanding.

These words echo in my mind if I raise my voice out loud. Some may look at me and say, "She's just crazy" if I just happen to break out and sing a simple melody.

What's strange is the world needs to be prepared for everything that I do. I am being unjustly judged by common standards alone and not by the silent pain I feel inside. Know that when I raise my voice it is not out of anger, that I raise my voice for one reason alone and that's only to be heard.

What Does it Matter to You?

What does it matter to you the way I wear my hair, the way I dress or the way I talk or how I walk? What does it matter to you the occupation that I have, the car I drive, or how much money I have?

What does it matter to you the contour of my body, the color of my skin, or the number of children I have? What business is it of yours whether I grew up in the country, the city or the suburbs; or whether I hail from New York, Paris, London or Dubai?

What does it matter to you if I ever went to jail, or whether my parents were married or not? Does it matter to you that I am married or single or gay or straight? Whose business is it that I am good or bad, light or dark skinned or what race I am.

What does it matter who I love or who loves me. Does it matter whether I eat healthy foods or not, or whether I immerse myself in a diet of junk foods? It actually is no business of yours.

What does matter to me is the way you treat me, or if you bully me or not. It matters to me when you disrespect me, lay your hands on me, or call me unsavory names. It matters to me when you hurt the people I love, and cause them to inflict pain on themselves.

What matters to me is when you steal from innocent people, and hurt the children, and victimize those who have done you no wrong.

These are the things that matter to me and they should matter to you. If we do all the wonderful gestures that matter, the world would be a better place. Realistically speaking it really does matter. It matters to the world.

I Know Not What To Say

I break my neck to hide the insecurities inside when all along I hold the key to my own destiny. The weary search to satisfy this yearning in my mind, is just an echo of my feelings that flows just like the tide.

As I go through life making needed changes along the way, there's still a voice so deep inside that knows not what to say.

The wind blows gently on top of the bay there's always times in life that we don't know which way to go.

But the karma that surrounds me will surely lead the way. My only hope and prayer to God is that I'll know just what to say.

Divinity

Divinity is what I seek within my soul, and I ask the help from Spirit to expand divinity to the world. Mere words cannot express the unlimited knowingness residing deep in me.

Divinity is quiet and still and eternally based on truth. Material things are illusions and at times appear so real. They have unimportance that as humans we cannot see.

Divinity transcends feelings high amidst the clouds it lies quietly making not a sound.

I don't know what my purpose is but soon it will be revealed. Divinity is like a web of life and soon my life will change.

I pray and meditate all I can to live life with smaller amounts of pain.

Divinity resides in me and in all of what I do. Divinity in purpose is my saving grace the only thing that I need to have is my faith.

Why Is It?

Why is that we care more about animals than mankind here on earth. Running out homeless people from the park when they need a place to sleep. We imprison people who hurt animals yet we make only a small attempt to try and help our young.

Why is it that we never offer our men and women food when they beg to only eat; yet we feed the pigeons food in the park? Why is it that hard working folk go broke after a hospital stay and little was done about women being beaten until important women began to die.

Why is it that society doesn't notice pain inside our kids until they become find love they seek within gangs and perpetrate shooting sprees. Our kids are crying out to be heard but few of us show them that we care. Berating neighbors and creating conflicts among ourselves is what's happening. Today our elderly are too afraid to show their faces in the day.

Why is it that disrespect has become the norm? It easier to be self absorbed and concerned with only self? Why is that we don't try harder to love each other anymore?

My Mothers Dress Tail

A little girl playing in a flower garden in a powder blue dress with black patent leather shoes on. Trying to keep her dress nice an clean.

She holds on to her mother's dress tail so she feels secure and won't get lost. The thought of being separated from her mother is upsetting to her. "Mama please don't leave me; she screams, Why are you so busy doing chores that you don't notice me." "Mother please slow down you walk too fast." You have dressed me like an angel and I know that you love me.

A little girl in a powder blue dress with black patent leather shoes is hanging onto her mother's dress tail. That little girl just happens to be me.

Trees

The trees of life blow gently as I watch and analyze the message that they bring to me. Trees blow fresh airs of hope, love and a most wonderful concept of togetherness. Trees that merge together share a closeness that few of us humans will ever know. Trees can never grow any taller than the size they are meant to be. They can never move away from one another and never travel anywhere.

Humans on the other hand are afforded so many luxuries and move around so freely yet we lack respect for each other. Trees touch each other gently or as directed by the wind. They never destroy, hate, or slaughter each other yet humans do all these things.

Trees are planted solid immovable, steadfastly cemented by nature in a place where they have no say. Trees have a way of being with each other accepting their fate. Trees remain together indefinitely; they accept life on its terms and live on until their season passes.

The Little Girl Inside of Me

The little girl inside of me is tired and needs to rest. Through all her years of struggling she has always done her very best.

Her views are so very fixed inside, for so many years oh my God has she cried.
She never learned to trust too deep for she knew what it involved.

Her mom was a victim of abuse that made her heart turn hard.

She is frightened of intimacy; its price seems much too high. For any man to walk all over her just like she is sand.

Now has come the time for her to get a long deserved rest. An honest and sincere relationship is what she hopes at best.

The new woman of the 90's is struggling to be free. With a better sense of whom she needs to be.

The letter girl inside of me has views that are obsolete. She will rid
herself of negativity so she can be complete.

Frostee Sharing at Wendy's

Two little kids sharing a Frostee at Wendy's it's no doubt that they are sister and brother. Sharing and patiently taking their turns.

No arguments, no fussing just sharing and passing the cup back and forth to one another.How wonderful to see them getting along so well, they act as if they each don't have a selfish bone in their body.

As an observer I wonder why mom just doesn't buy another Frostee so they each have their own? Maybe their moms on a budget and can only afford one, or it could be that maybe learning to share with each other is the lesson their mother wants them to learn?

Now they are taking a break from eating, and happily place the Frostee in front of mom. Looking at them really warmed my heart, because I realized that they had saved a nice amount of Frostee for mom. How sweet!

As they begin to chat with each other, happily laughing and communicating in a loving way. It was such a joy for me to see. Two kids sharing a Frostee at Wendy's what a sight to behold. It makes me feel joyful that I had the blissful pleasure of being there.

No One Knows my Secret Thoughts but Me

No one knows my secret thoughts but me which lurk in the background waiting for a chance to overtake my mind.

A million ideas and thoughts detonate in my psyche that I can't control. Good thoughts and bad but the bad seem to outweigh the good. It draws me like a hypnotic daydream resonating in my heart.

The aching pain at the loss of you I'm told gets duller each and every day. I have loved truly only once in my life and it filled my life with such intense excitement and pain. It's a love pain and it takes time to heal.

Endings seem so permanent to me yet there is no real permanency at all, I wish it were only an illusion. A love pain awakens me from my sleep and takes my appetite away. My body aches for you and I can't take the strain, I'm lost in the crevices of my mind and have no place to hide.

God please don't let me love someone who does not love me. That would be a grave catastrophe. Shakespeare words echo in my mind. "It is better to have loved and lost then not to have loved at all." I wonder sometimes. I'm so very thankful that no one really knows my secret thoughts but me.

I'm told that a love pain has an ending time but the pain seems like it will never end. My days and nights all seem the same, but I know it's for a greater gain. I keep telling myself it will be over soon I'm sure my creator will see me through. Among other things I am thankful that no one really knows my secret thoughts but me.

Understanding

Sometimes I feel I just started and I'm facing the end.
Sometimes I feel like God's coldhearted because he's taken my friends. But I read between the lines and record the message. Problems come for a reason live and learn the lessons.

There's ups and down in life either you're happy or sad. But you have to learn to take the good with the bad. I'm getting old in age so its forget the games. But it's hard to love a woman because love is pain. It hurts my brain but I'm so use to the pain I can't feel it. Is my life full of fake people and I'm the realest thing is my life? I can't make any mistakes.

I never play a bad hand I always hold an Ace. And be patient good things happen to those who wait. Time separates the real so you know the fakes. You don't need a fortune teller to be told your fate. Just pray your mistakes make you wiser with years and believe half what you see and not what you hear. And always take your time to prepare what you do, because the trees that grow slow always bear the best fruit.

- Jamie Roshaud Woods

Innocent Love

Innocent love is what I feel when I am with you and the width and depth of the earth seems endless. Innocent love is what I feel when I look in your face I am ignited by the passion in your eyes. And after hearing the sound of your voice.

Innocent love is what I feel when I surrender my love to you and give of myself from the very deepness of my heart and soul. Innocent love is what I feel when you promise to keep a smile on my face and never hurt me. This regrettably turns out to be an untruth. The hurt that you perpetrated caused me to cry a river of many tears. Innocent love is what I feel each day that I am away from you and I miss you more and more each day.

Innocent love is what I sense when you tell me it's over and you've decide to look for something more. Innocent love is what I feel when I beg you to stay with me and you decide to leave me anyway. Innocent love is what I feel when I vow never to give my heart to anyone again. Innocent love is what I feel when my heart feels like it's going to burst open in my chest because I love you so much.

Innocent love is what I feel when I must let go of you in order to keep my dignity and self esteem. Innocent love is what I feel when we have come to the end and I don't want to let you go but know I must give you up to save me. Innocent love is what I feel when I can say to myself that you don't love me anymore and I still love you. Innocent love is what I fed when I go through the pain and fear to find love again.

- Dedicated to Wesley

I Can Choose the Things I like

I can choose the things I like now. I don't have to eat the foods I didn't like when I was as child. I don't have to be in places and with people I don't like anymore. I don't have to say things I don't mean anymore. I don't have to smile and laugh when I don't want to anymore. I can choose the things I like and don't feel guilty anymore.

I don't have to stand for abuse anymore because I feel too insecure. I can choose the things I like and assert myself and be willing to make changes if I like.

I can choose the partner I want to love, raise my children they way I like and surround myself with enlightened people if I want. I can choose the things I like now and be the greatest person I wish to be right now. Today.

Rodney King

Rodney King, oh Rodney King I know you are so tired. You were once a victim until you were put on trial.

What did the police officers say to you word-for-word yells the prosecuting attorney who doesn't want you to be heard.
People often ask you why you lied to the police.

Because you were already labeled all your cards were on the table.
It's hard to believe Rodney that you would tackle the police when you know how difficult it is from being on the streets.

Rodney King, oh Rodney King you have been wounded deep inside. Our children will read about you in your life before you die.

We never really told you Rodney, that you are a very special guy. Who truly believed that justice would ring out into the sky.

In the midst of turmoil Rodney you have shown us what we need. We need to love each other more in order to succeed.

If You Saw Her

If you saw her today tomorrow you'd see her everywhere.
When she smiles you see a glimpse of everyone's face that lives.
Her smile is like the sun peeking though the clouds after the rain
on a hot summer day.

Her charm pulls an admirer like quicksand submerging its
victim.
The lady is a delight to see because she is a part of yesterday, today
tomorrow and forever.

When she cries or mourns all who hear her beckon to her call.
And when she is joyful, her joy makes love to you.
Like a mother nursing a newborn child. Life is her name.
Touch her and know the beauty and Joy of living.

Dedicated to Frank Wilson

Frosty Gray Sky

Frosty gray; that is the color of the sky today as I sit and listen to the rain pattering against the windows of my car. The frosty gray sky is not depressing at all to me; there is a beauty that exits, a character, a symbol a message. I wish I could go to sleep, wake up, and the world would be safe and people would not have to live in fear; where the rich didn't take advantage of the poor, and kids didn't have to grow up so fast.

Where elders are respected not thrown into nursing homes to perish and wither away, and parenting is a joy not a inconvenience. Where families are families again, and we stop cheating and fighting for money and power.

Frosty gray skies help me forget that fewer and fewer people really care with the belief that tomorrow will be different than today. Frosty gray skies help me accept that today is the day; that change is on the way. I only pray that God blesses me with his grace and the opportunity to see it before I take my last breath.

The Art of Gentle Persuasion

A man chases a woman until he claims her for his own. He whispers sweet nothings into her ear, telephones her, emails and texts her at all times of the night; for no other reason than to let her know he cares. That's the art of gentle persuasion and he shows her in such a loving way.

A man chases a woman with the intent of being her one and only man; without knowing if it they will be a match. Other times, he knows that she will be his for eternity. His thoughts are only of her and he revels just being in her presence. The funny laugh she has, the way her face lights up when she's happy. And when she is downhearted because the world has not been kind, he is right there to lift her up to the clouds. That's the art of gentle persuasion and he does it in such a focused way.

A man chases a woman until he secures her love, he doesn't really understand her completely, but that's ok with him. He is her protector, her knight in shinning armor, who shelters her from the uncertainties that life often holds. That's the art of gentle persuasion and he demonstrates his love from his heart.

A man chases the woman he has fallen in love with, not to control her, not to abuse her, lie and deceive her, but to claim her for his own. He recognizes the jewel that she is and is not ashamed to let the world know that she is his alone. That's the art of gentle persuasion and he stands out from the crowd. He is on top of his game. Only a real man appreciates the gifts that she has. That's the Art of Gentle Persuasion.

Momma Knows Best

In the stillness of the night I toss and turn while everyone else sleeps; but alas, cannot. My mind is active, racing, worrying about my son. While he was growing up he never was a problem, never got into trouble, never spent time in Juvenile Hall.

He sits not in prison because of the decisions he has made. I taught him the challenges of growing up in a society where a man is accused because of the color of his skin. I cautioned him about the company that you keep, and taught him to believe in a *Higher Power* that watches and protects us all from wrong. If only he had believed because momma really knows best. Now I am serving a sentence outside wondering what I did wrong, what could I have done to prevent this atrocity.

I feel as if I have lost my freedom. Who will be there to comfort and love him the way that I do? Life is not the same for me. Momma knows best but God is more knowledgeable than I am, or could ever be.

Lulu Is Her Name

Men and women come to the nail shop to get their feet manicured but that's not all that they receive. They receive love, understanding, and direction while their toes are being taken care of. They come not knowing that their hearts are heavy and burdened by life. Once she begins massaging their feet, they begin to share their fears: problems with children, and relatives who show them no love; in a world that shows little mercy to them.

Lulu is her name and giving hope to others is her claim. She is not rich in material possessions, but her wealth exudes from a deep place inside of her spirit. Lulu is her name, she is an angel sent from heaven. She is not really here to care for the feet but to care for the soul. Lulu is her name.

Mother Nature

In the middle of a crowd I blend; enmeshed in the delight of being connected to the earth. The sun settles behind the mountains and I am captured by serenity and closeness to mother nature, the stars, the air, the grass, dirt and the insects the pests they often are.

I am reminded of a stage play and a familiar melody that speaks to me in a private way. I am honored that spirit has blessed me with the ability to enjoy this revelation that mother nature offers to me. Yet I often forget to be grateful for the smallest of things.

As a child I was in touch with Mother Nature. I felt the dirt under my feet and on my hands. As an adult it seems very different now, and I have little time to be with Mother Nature. Why is that? Mother Nature is only visible if I take the time to connect with her. She outstretches her arms to me with love.

A Lawnmower

The effervescent sun shines brightly even through the dark skies It's such a beautiful day as I pause to hear the sounds of someone mowing their lawn.

The lawnmower rattles, shakes, and stammers until it catches and a steady sound beings to emit from it. It must be ready to do its job; to mow the lawn.

No matter how miniscule it seems to others, it brings me a feeling of joy. Some would say its just a lawnmower what's the big deal? The sound of it lets me know that the grass will soon be chopped.

The smell of fresh grass sharpens my senses and makes me feel grateful to be alive; the sound is magic to my ears. A lawnmower reminds me that I am alive and to live life each day of the week being grateful.

Mama What We Gonna Do?

Tonight is really cold mama and we have no place to go. Seems we have run out of places to stay, so mama, what we gonna do? The night is dark and scary and no one is willing to share a space for us to sleep. We are homeless again mama, what happened?

What we gonna do mama, when you have broken all the rules and no one wants to give us another chance. Wherever we go you get into trouble by making someone angry, and we have to leave. Mama, what we gonna do? The little money that you receive each and every month just evaporates into thin air. Mama, you have a problem with drugs and are unwilling to face this demon so we all must suffer. You promise us over and over again that you will change.

You tell us that we will have our own house and we won't have to live from pillar to post. All are broken promises that never seem to come true. Mama, what we gonna do? I can't take this stress much longer. I am way too young to worry the way that I do.

Mama, what we gonna do? I am carrying your burdens, and I can't take it anymore; Mama I wish many times that you were different and could take care of us like you did before.

Mama, what we gonna do? I am just a kid, and these problems are too much for me to bear. Please mama, take over your job and set this little girl free. You know that I love you no matter what you do. Your my mother and I love you so please do the best you can.